Science
START HERE!

MAKING IT MOVE

Simple models to build on, from Central Television's schools television series, Science – Start Here!

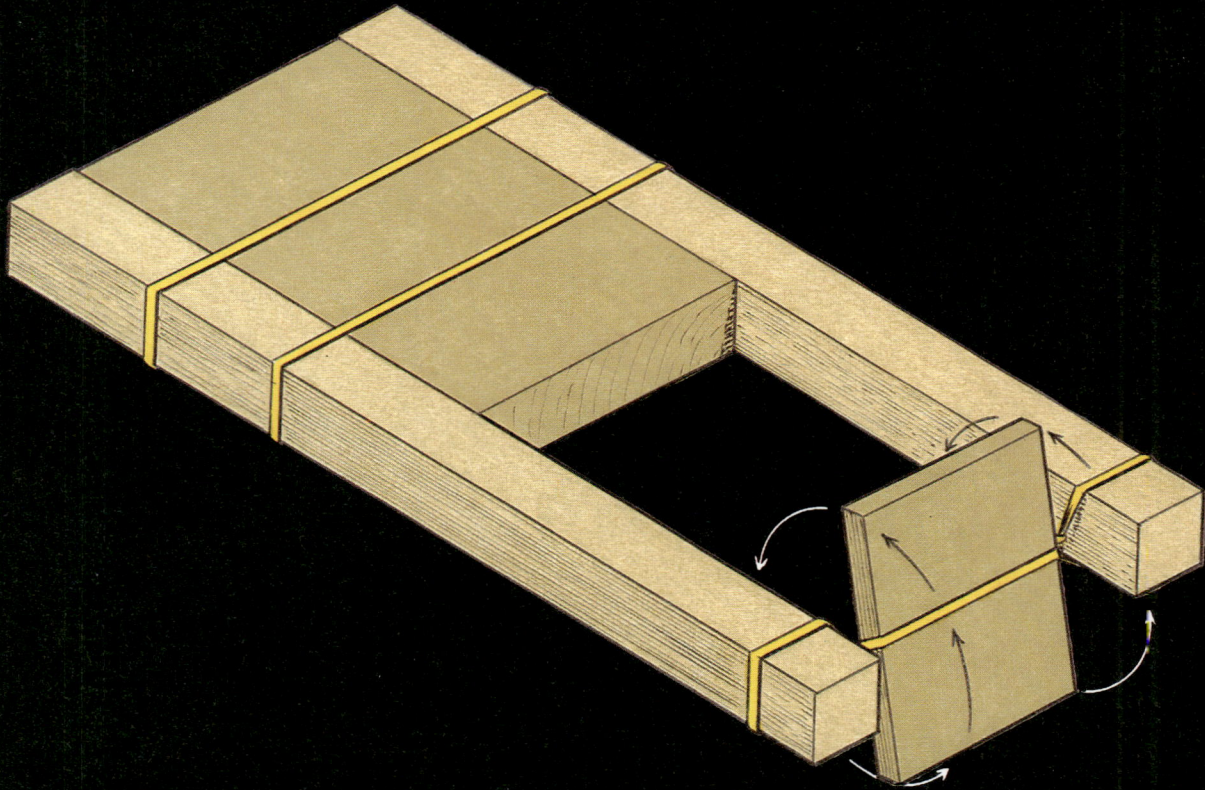

John Stringer

Nelson

Making it Move is based on programmes in the *Science – Start Here!*
television series for schools produced by Central Independent Television plc.

Thomas Nelson and Sons Ltd
Nelson House   Mayfield Road   Walton-on-Thames
Surrey   KT12 5PL   UK

51 York Place   Edinburgh   EH1 3JD   UK

Thomas Nelson (Hong Kong) Ltd
Toppan Building 10/F   22A Westlands Road
Quarry Bay   Hong Kong

Thomas Nelson Australia
102 Dodds Street   South Melbourne   Victoria 3205   Australia

Nelson Canada
1120 Birchmount Road   Scarborough   Ontario
M1K 5G4   Canada

© **John Stringer**

Science – Start Here!
logo and programme material

© 1987, 1988 Central Independent Television plc

First published by Thomas Nelson and Sons Ltd 1988

ISBN 0-17-423102-4
NPN 987654

Printed in Hong Kong

Acknowledgements

Many of the practical ideas in this book were devised and developed by Harry Starkey, CDT Adviser, City of Coventry, and his inspiration and encouragement are gratefully acknowledged.

The publishers would like to thank the following organisations and individuals for permission to reproduce the photographs and archive material in this book:

Heather Angel p12 top right; Barnaby's Picture Library p19 bottom; Alastair Black p27 top left; Dept. Medical Illustration, St. Bartholomew's Hospital p18 lower right; L. Campbell/NHPA, front cover left; J. Allan Cash p13 top left, p14 top left, p25 top, p26 bottom right; Central Independent Television plc p8 top right; Gunter Ziesler (Bruce Coleman) p6 left: Colorific p4 left and right; Richard Crawford p19 top; Mary Evans Picture Library p7 top left and right, p10 left, p15 top left; Frank Lane Picture Agency p6 right, p12 left; Robert Harding p10 bottom right; Hong Kong Tourist Authority p17 top left; MJ Hooks p14 lower left; Mansell Collection p26 top left and top right; Chris Perrett p18 top right, p25 bottom, p28; Ann Ronan Picture Library p26 bottom left; Science Photo Library p17 top right; Tony Stone Associates, front cover right, p5; Bob Watkins p15 lower left, p18 bottom left; Klaus Benser (ZEFA) p29 top left.

Illustrations and diagrams by David Tanner and Richard Crawford Graphic Design.

Contents
Ideas developed in each section of this book

FLIGHT   6

Birds and some other animals can fly. People have tried to copy them.

Certain shapes will lift up when pushed, pulled or dropped through the air. Only some shapes fly well.

Certain materials are better for flying machines than others. How you shape the materials is of great importance for successful, controlled flight.

MACHINES   18

'Machine' is a word that we can use for very simple devices that make work easier.

There are five simple machines – the lever, the ramp, the screw, the wheel and axle, and the pulley.

Simple machines can 'amplify' the force of our hands, arms, and legs, or of other mechanical devices.

Energy can be transmitted through cogs, chains, shafts and bands.

By reducing the loss of energy through friction, we can make some machines more efficient.

SHIPSHAPE   26

We have developed a range of different ways of travelling through water.

Hull shape, loading, motive power, and sail type (where appropriate) can make a difference to the efficiency and performance of a boat.

Boats must be *carefully* loaded for stability.

For parents and teachers

What's so important about learning science? Why is it considered to be a vital part of the primary school curriculum?

The HMI Science Committee said:

> Science, with its emphasis on the study of the environment and concern for direct observation and practical investigation, matches what we know of how children learn.
>
> It can assist pupils to bring questioning minds to their experience of things around them. The teaching of science should seek to develop the processes of scientific thinking.

Science is important because:

- we live in a scientific world.

- children should be encouraged to be aware of their environment, to be interested in its richness and to experience the excitement of recognising its possibilities.

- it helps children develop respect for the world and its inhabitants, understanding that their responsible and humane behaviour can make it a better and more interesting place for all.

- we have a custodial responsibility to care for the land, sea and air, and should leave them better after our presence, understanding our dependency on other forms of life.

- children are naturally curious and we, as adults, should encourage this questioning. The questions are as important as the answers.

- above all, science is fun and enjoyable – let's encourage children to appreciate and enjoy their world.

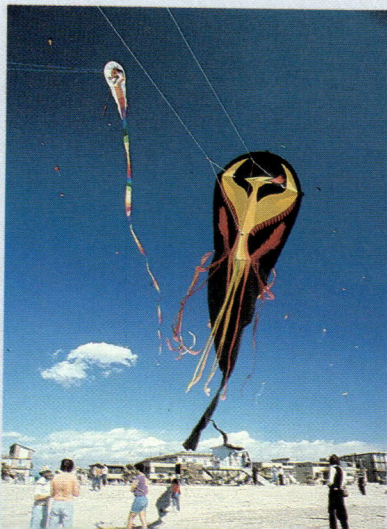

The *Science – Start Here!* books aim to present scientific activities that are:

- relevant and interesting to children.
- building on children's everyday experiences.
- encouraging active classroom and home investigations.
- helping to develop children's scientific skills.

What are these scientific skills? They include the ability to:

- observe carefully, sort and classify.
- ask questions of the 'What would happen if . . .?' sort.
- suggest explanations and make guesses based on observations.
- design investigations and experiments.
- prepare and use apparatus.
- measure accurately, *although children should be encouraged to estimate* before measuring.
- make decisions on the basis of evidence.
- develop concepts and knowledge. There are fundamental concepts in science, and *Science – Start Here!* embodies many of these and introduces a body of knowledge through which to practise these skills.
- communicate findings. *Science – Start Here!* introduces activities that will encourage children to communicate their findings through discussion, illustration, displays and the written word.
- apply knowledge to new situations.

The subject areas of the books match the broad areas of investigation recognised by the DES in *Science 5–16: A statement of policy* (1985). They are:

- living things and their interaction with the environment.
- materials and their characteristics.
- energy and materials.
- forces and their effects.

This book aims to relate simple activities and model-making to real life; pictures from our environment – or from history – have been chosen to reflect practical application.

It asks a number of questions which children can answer, and have answered, in a range of original ways. Don't always feel that you have to have the answers – or indeed, that you have to give them!

As far as possible, *Making it Move* uses materials that are available or easily obtainable at school or at home. Few additional materials are necessary, but some of the following are needed for one – or occasionally more – model:

florist's soft wire.	sheet of sandpaper.
wooden kebab skewers.	small carpet square.
pea sticks or thin dowel rod.	tall plastic cups.
balloons – round and long.	soft scrap wood or balsa offcuts.
washing-up liquid bottles.	few large nails.
length of foam pipe insulation from a D.I.Y. shop.	small wood screws, or small nuts and bolts.
	screw 'eyes'.

For a few activities, it is necessary to cut soft wood or the foam pipe insulation. A junior hacksaw (the wire frame type) is recommended – **not** a sharp knife. The material to be cut can be held still with a bench hook, which protects both table and fingers.

For many of the materials, there are acceptable alternatives; often, children will think of better ones than you! If their alternative doesn't work, that, too, is a learning experience – but don't let it lead to frustration.

Note: **The activities in this book have been used with safety and success by many children of primary school age. Nevertheless, parents and teachers are advised to give careful consideration to the supervision of practical work, and to follow the explicit safety instructions given in the text.**

FLIGHT

We have always envied the way birds fly. But we don't have the muscles or the light, delicate skeleton of birds. We have had to design and make machines to lift us into the sky.

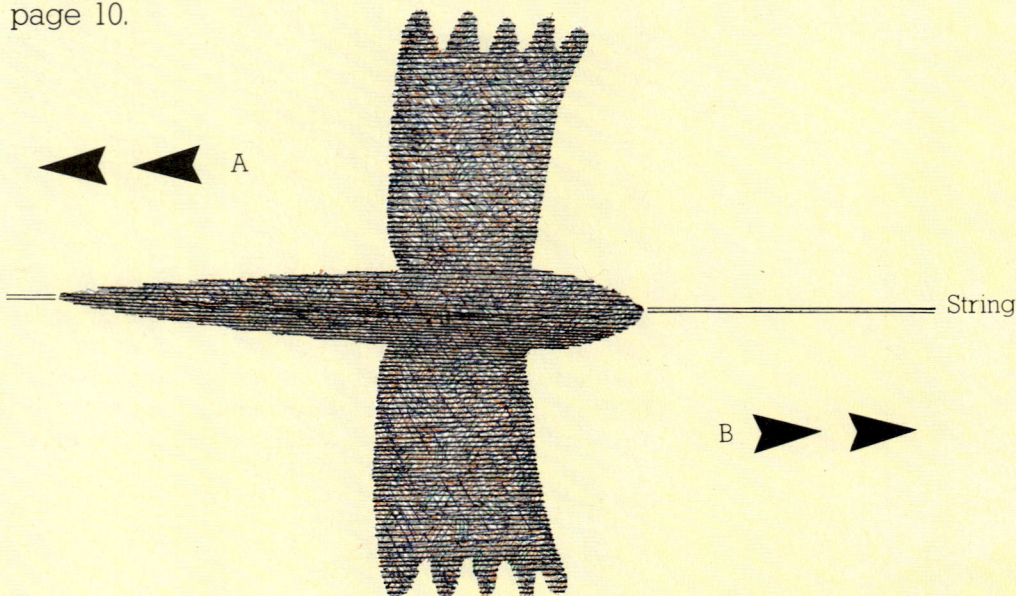

Humming birds can beat their wings 60 times a second. They can hover, and fly backwards.

Left. The condor's wide wings help it soar high above the mountains.

Different birds fly in different ways. Think about their shapes and what their wings look like.

This is a 'two-way' bird. Moved one way, it looks like a harmless goose, with a long neck and short tail. Moved the other way, it looks like a hunting bird of prey, with a short neck and long tail. This shape, made into a kite, frightens birds eating crops – so long as it is the right way up! It then becomes a flying scarecrow – see page 10.

A

String

B

We have tried many ways of flying like a bird.

The Wright brothers are thought to have been the first to design and build a successful heavier-than-air flying machine.

Samuel Cody built kites large enough to carry people.

Going up!

Take a sheet of paper and twist the edge under. Blow gently across the top.

What happens?

What happens when you vary the force of your blowing? Can you make the paper rise and fall?

Look at the pictures of aeroplanes and birds in this book. Can you see how your paper looks like a wing?

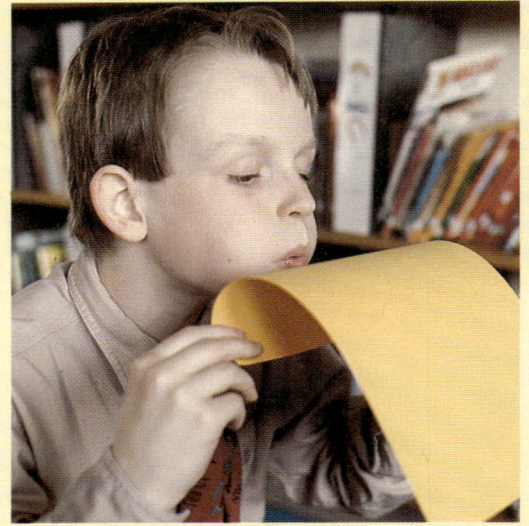

Make this model wing, using stiff paper. Carefully, make a hole right through it, and glue in a piece of drinking straw. Add a stiff paper tail. Thread it onto a string or thin wire.

Blow across your model wing. Blow gently, then harder, then from different angles.

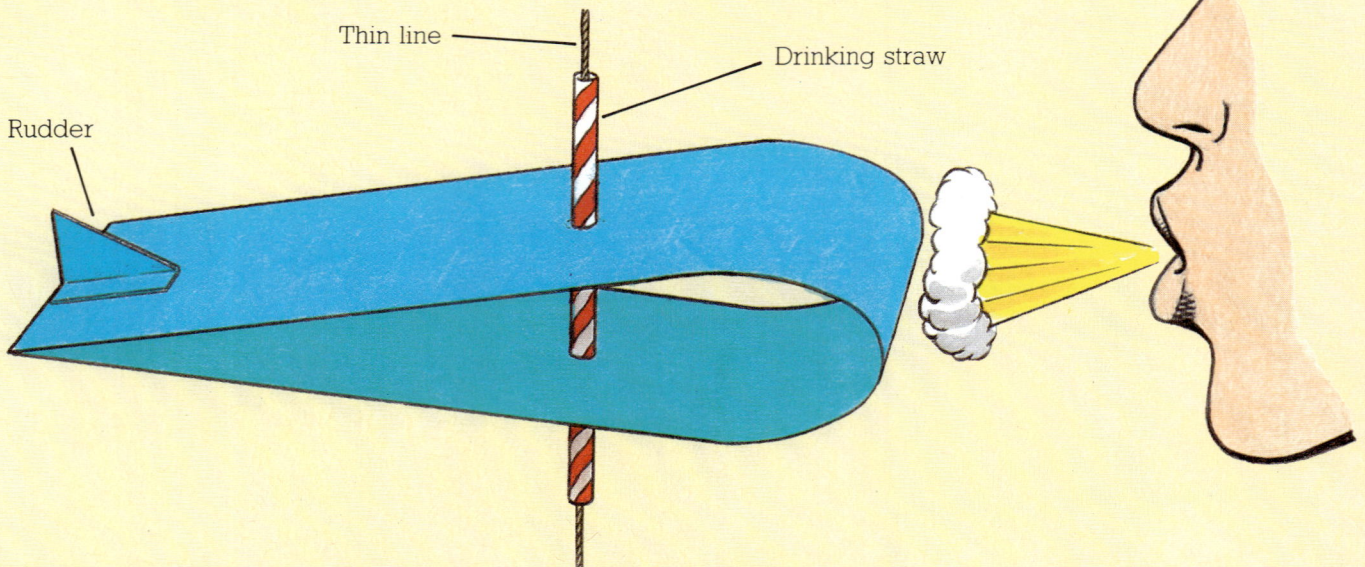

Thin line

Drinking straw

Rudder

What happens?

What is the tail for? Try the wing without it.

The air moving across the top of an aeroplane's wing presses more lightly than the air below it. The wing begins to lift. Did you feel that lift in your model wings?

Flight commander

Make a paper dart. Try adding weight to the nose (a small paper clip). If it stalls, add more weight. If it dives, take weight away. Can you make your dart fly on a smooth, straight course?

This picture shows control surfaces on a paper dart.

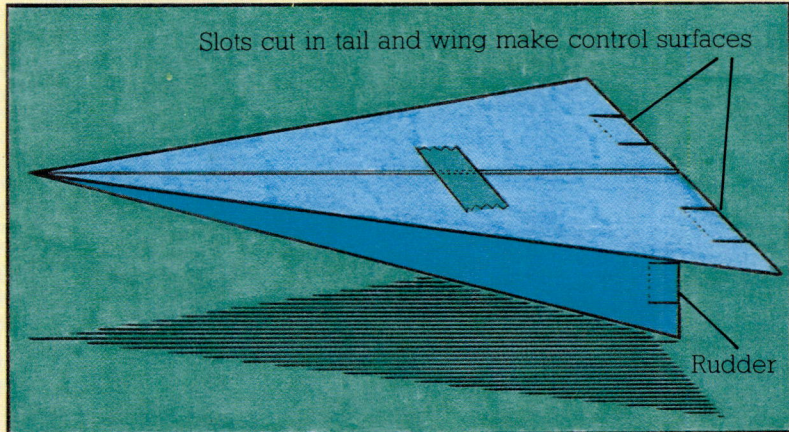

Slots cut in tail and wing make control surfaces

Rudder

Cut control surfaces on your dart. Try bending them slightly. Can you make your dart:

    turn to the left?   turn to the right?

    climb?   dive?

Now try some simple games, using paper darts with control surfaces. Make them:

fly in a half circle.

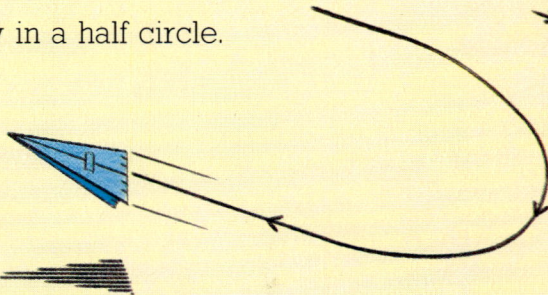

land between two lines drawn on the ground.

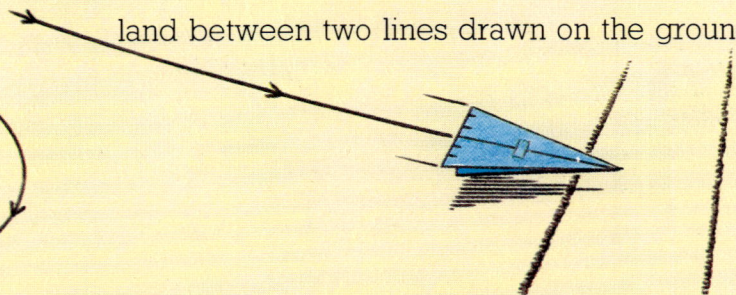

land in a ring on the ground.

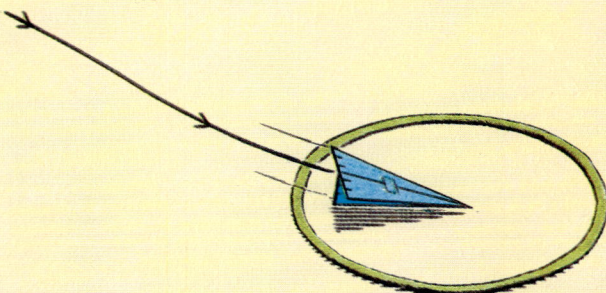

fly through a hoop or ring held 5m away from you.

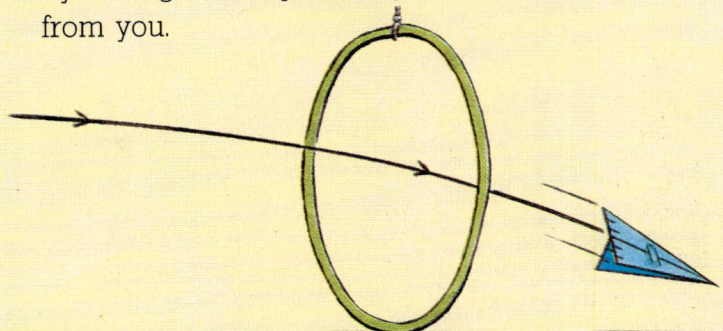

**NEVER CLIMB TO LAUNCH YOUR PAPER DART.
NEVER FLY IT NEAR ROADS OR WATER.**

Kites

You may know some different sorts of kite already. A traditional box kite is made with cotton, wood and string. A Ferrari kite has no struts. The wind, blowing through its tubes, gives it a shape.

Page 6 shows a kite used by farmers to scare birds from their crops. It looks like a bird of prey.

These are stunt kites, each with two strings. Stunt kites climb, dive and loop, under control.

Children in many countries have played with kites for hundreds of years.

Build a kite

Use the lightest carrier bag you can find. You could use the fine plastic that wraps dry-cleaning – but only with adult help. Plastic bags can be dangerous.

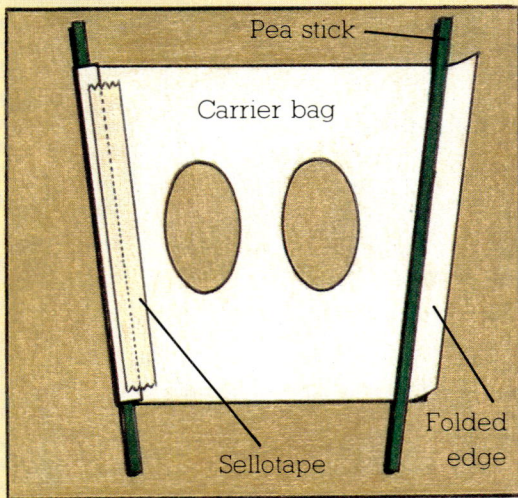

Cut the plastic bag into the shape shown on the left. Two holes sometimes help the kite fly.

Fold two pea sticks into the side edges. Stick the edges down with tape.

Fasten four short strings – all the same length – as shown below. Tie them all together to make the harness.

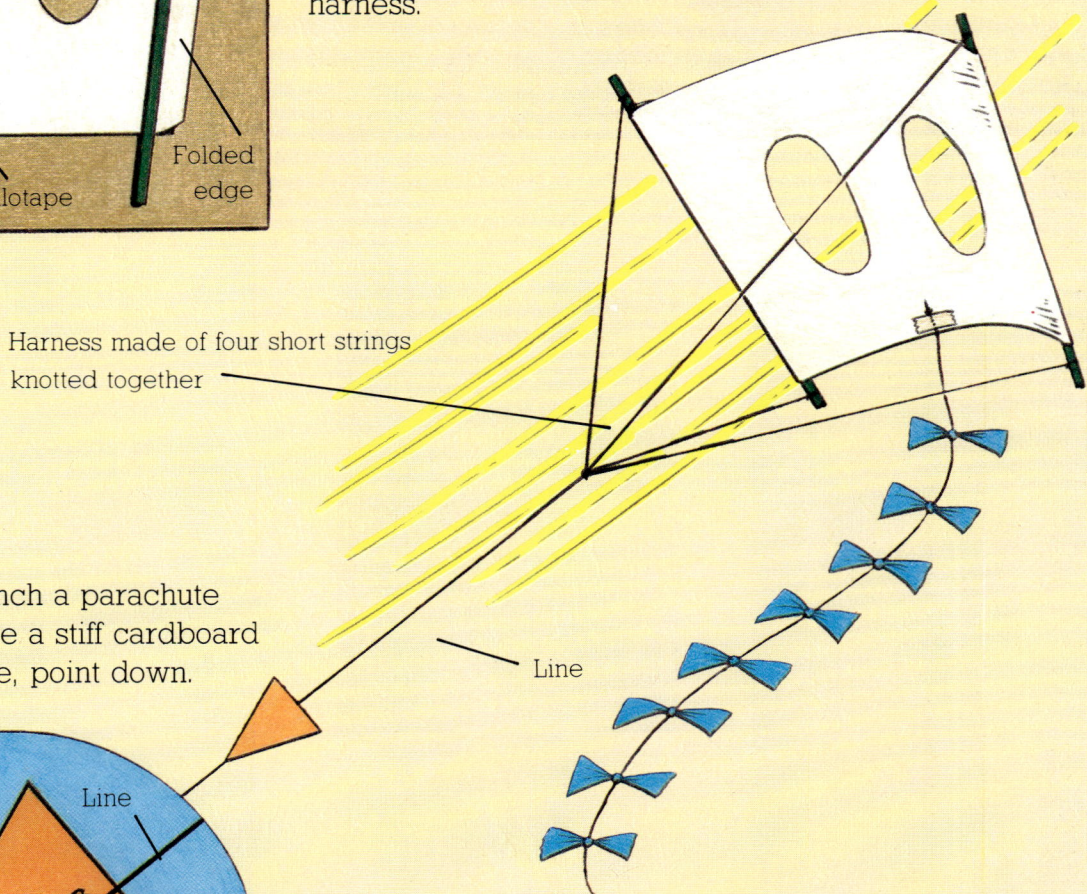

Pea stick

Carrier bag

Sellotape

Folded edge

Harness made of four short strings knotted together

Line

If you wish to launch a parachute (see page 13) tape a stiff cardboard triangle to the line, point down.

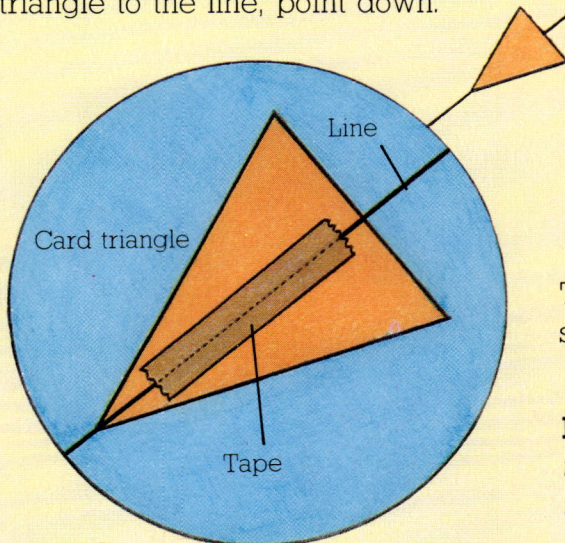

Line

Card triangle

Tape

The kite may fly better with a tail, made by knotting scrap pieces of plastic bag into a string.

Launch tip: *You need a good wind, and a friend to throw your kite as you keep jerking the line. Shorten the lower strings of the harness if the wind is gentle.*

NEVER FLY KITES NEAR ELECTRICITY CABLES OR PYLONS, OR OVER ROADS.

Spinning down

Many plants have flying, or floating, fruits and seeds. The wind carries them so that new plants can grow away from their parents.

They are likely to fly further the longer they can stay up, or the taller the plant.

Sycamore fruits grow in pairs. Sometimes they break up into single fruits. Which flies better – a pair of fruits or a single one?

Use a piece of stiff paper, about 20 cm by 10 cm, to make a gyrocopter as shown below. Weight it with a paperclip. Throw it up from the ground.

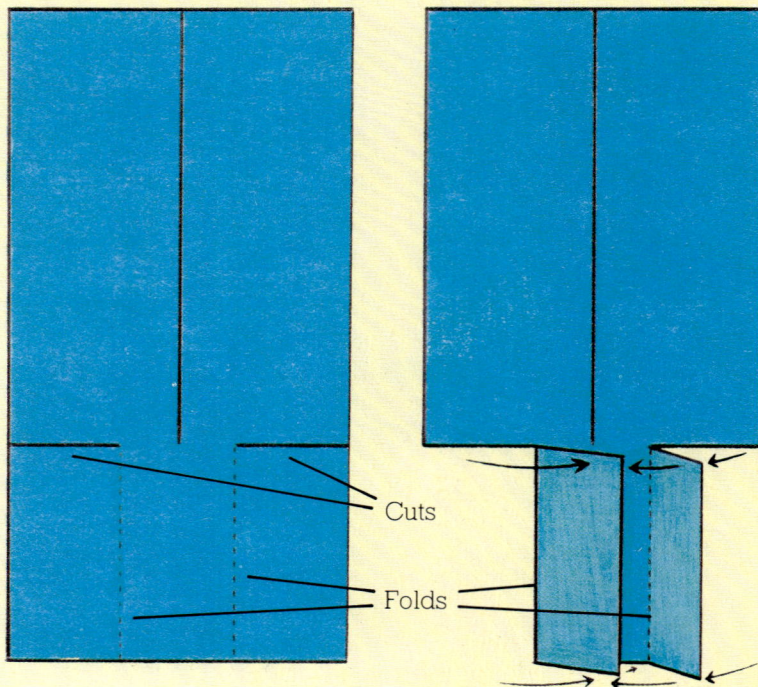

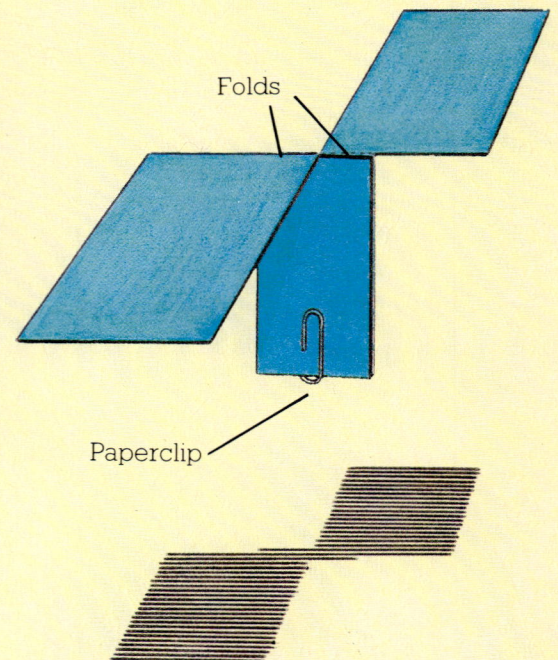

Cuts

Folds

Folds

Paperclip

Can you make it:

    spiral left?

    spiral right?

Can you make gyrocopters that will:

    fall very slowly?

    fall very fast but still spiral?

    land in a 'target area'?

NEVER CLIMB TO LAUNCH YOUR GYROCOPTER.

Floating down

You can make parachutes with tissue paper and thread.

Glue the threads to tissue paper triangles – sticky tape doesn't hold well.

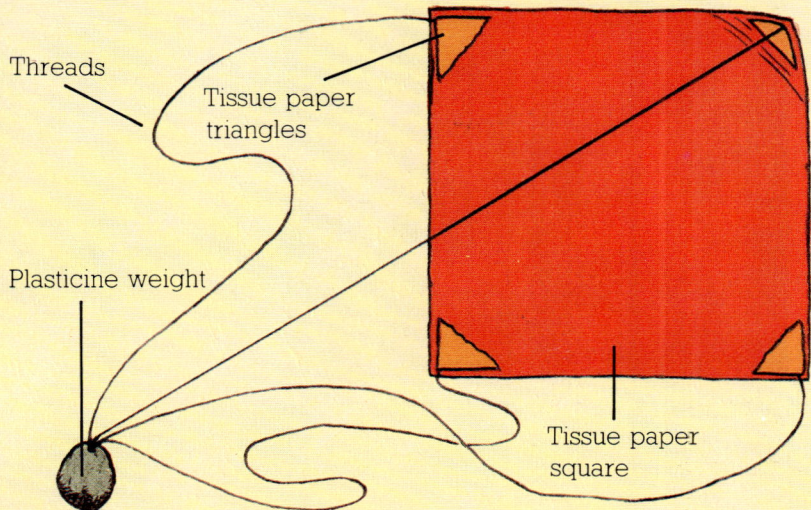

Threads

Tissue paper triangles

Plasticine weight

Tissue paper square

Launch the parachute folded or lightly crumpled up. Wrap the weight in the middle, so that you can throw it high.

Try launching it from a kite. Tape a card triangle to the line (see page 6) and make a paperclip hook. Put the open parachute on the line of the flying kite and let it slide up. The triangle should release it.

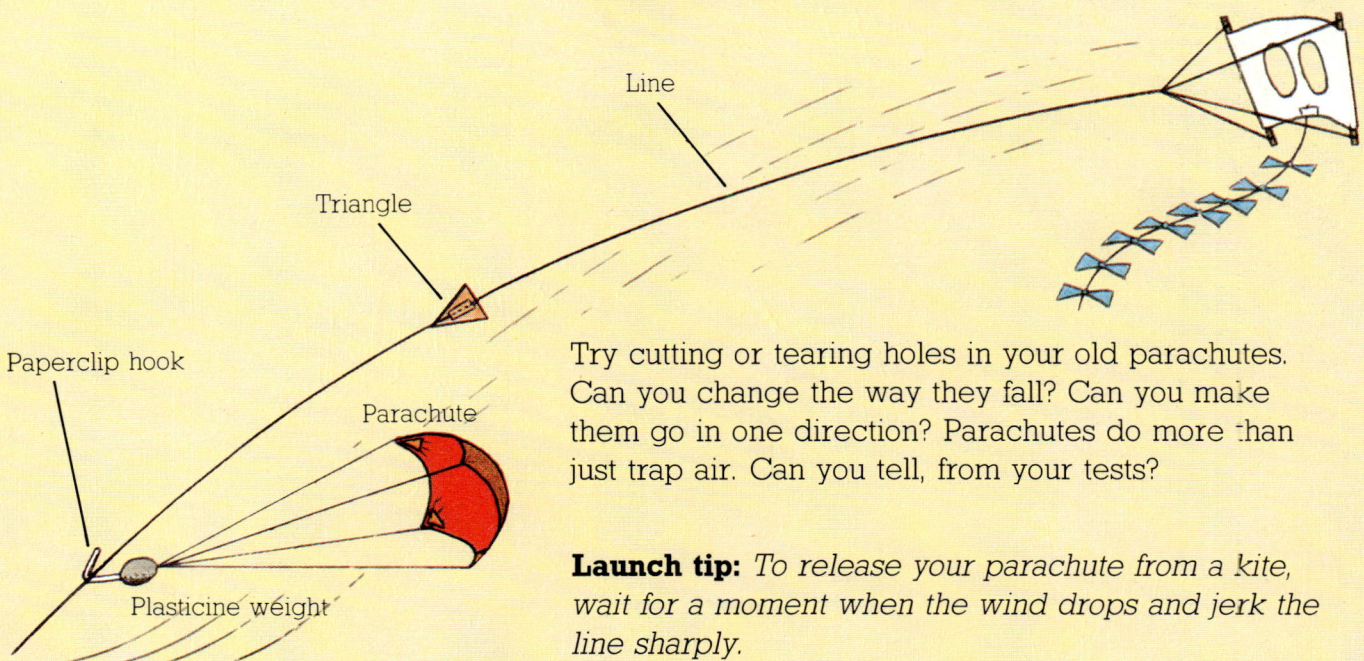

Line

Triangle

Paperclip hook

Parachute

Plasticine weight

Try cutting or tearing holes in your old parachutes. Can you change the way they fall? Can you make them go in one direction? Parachutes do more than just trap air. Can you tell, from your tests?

Launch tip: *To release your parachute from a kite, wait for a moment when the wind drops and jerk the line sharply.*

NEVER CLIMB OR LEAN FROM A HEIGHT TO LAUNCH YOUR PARACHUTE.

Spinning up

Helicopters can hover to make rescues.

Birotor helicopters can lift great weights.

Cut a strip from an old plastic bottle. Carefully make a small hole in the centre.

Give the strip a good twist. (Warm it on the radiator first.) Push a wooden skewer through the hole. *Glue it firmly.*

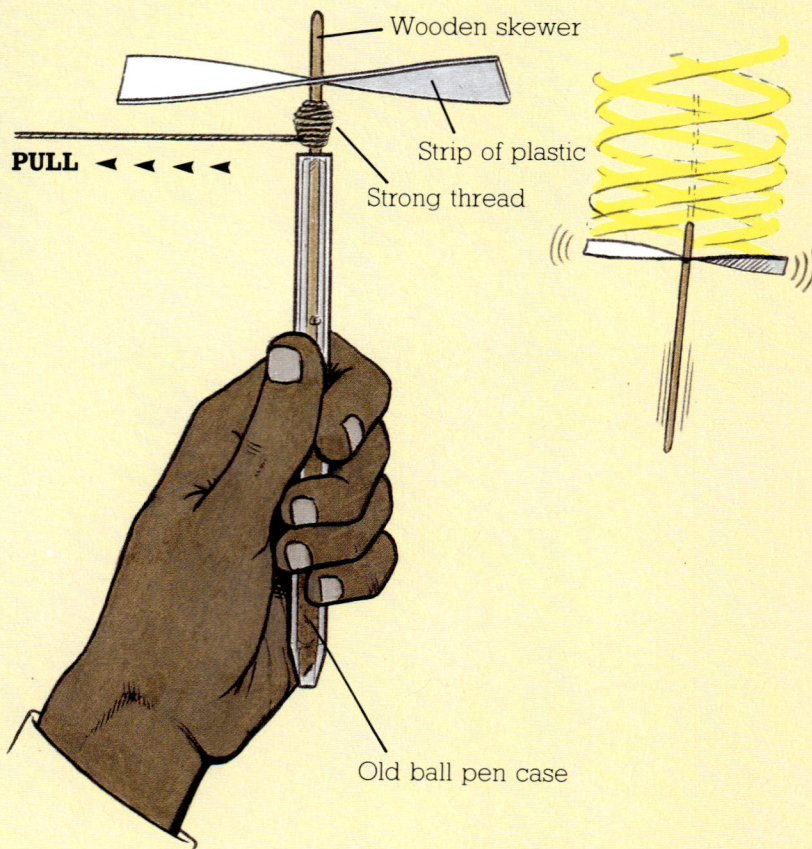

Wooden skewer

Strip of plastic

Strong thread

PULL ◄ ◄ ◄ ◄

Old ball pen case

You can spin the helicopter between your palms, or make a launcher from an old ball pen case. Wind a strong thread round the skewer, without tying. Hold the tube firmly. Pull the thread sharply.

If your helicopter won't fly, look carefully at how you wind on the thread, and the shape of the plastic rotor.

Can you make a helicopter with *two* rotors? Try them one above the other – or in a cross. Which is better?

Does a helicopter with two rotors fly better?

Launch tip: *Two cup hooks in a stake pushed in the ground make a stronger launcher.*

Floating up

Scientists who saw smoke rising above a fire thought that a bag full of smoke would rise. But smoke is only dust carried up by hot air.

The Montgolfier brothers used hot air to lift people into the sky.

Some gases are lighter than the air, and rise upward. If you put them in a bag, they take the bag up, too. These gas balloons may contain hydrogen (a dangerous gas that burns) or helium (a safe gas).

Airships are cigar-shaped. They may contain lots of separate gas chambers. The cabin may have an engine and propeller to drive the airship.

Flying balloon models are not safe. They involve gases or fire. Only the helium balloons you can buy (already filled) are safe.

But you can make model balloons to look at and enjoy. Use toy balloons, and thin strips of cardboard rather than thread.

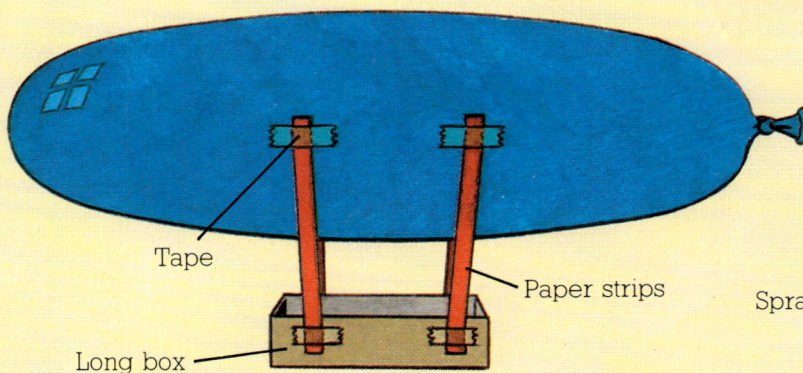

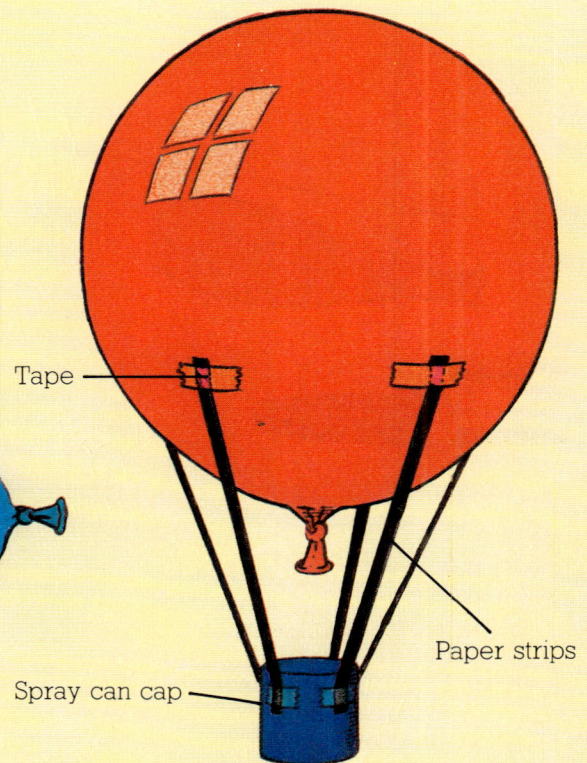

Tape

Paper strips

Spray can cap

Tape

Paper strips

Long box

Riding on air

Hovercraft float on a cushion of air made by huge fans turned by their motors. The hovercraft was invented by Sir Christopher Cockerell. Early ones were very simple.

In remote parts of the world, hovercraft can carry in supplies because they travel over land *and* water.

Make a small hole in a plastic ceiling tile. Using a junior hacksaw, trim a ball pen top as shown, to make a tapering tube. Glue this into your ceiling tile.

Ceiling tile

Tail cut off

Top cut off

Tape

Pen top pushed through

Slip the neck of a round balloon over the pen top. You may need to wrap it firmly with tape. Blow up the balloon through the pen top.

You could try a cheese box instead of a tile.

Can you make a hovercraft that hovers *longer*?

Does your tile hovercraft work on water?

Rocket power

The Chinese have been enjoying firework rockets for thousands of years.

Rockets have no moving parts. They use fuel to produce a massive amount of gas, which is forced out backwards through a nozzle. This pushes the rocket forward – or upward. Rockets can power planes and space ships, and carry lines from lifeboats to ships in trouble.

Rockets – especially firework rockets – are dangerous. Try this safe indoor rocket.

Blow up a long balloon, twist the end, and hold it closed with a clothes peg.

Use two strips of tape to attach it to a piece of drinking straw, threaded onto a line stretched across the room.

Release the clothes peg.

Tape

Drinking straw

Thin line

How far will your rocket travel?

Can you increase the distance?

Will a paper fin, taped on, make the 'flight' smoother and more controlled?

What is your rocket fuel?

MACHINES

We often think of machines as big complicated devices, full of cogs or electronics. But a machine is anything that makes work easier. For example:

A **lever** makes it easier to move things. It can make that movement stronger, or weaker. It can change its direction. A seesaw is a machine, when you rock it to and fro as a big lever.

A **ramp** makes it easier to move heavy loads upwards. By lifting toys on wheels to the top of ramps, you put energy into them that makes them run down when you let go! A ramp is a machine when you use it to lift a car.

A **screw** is like a long ramp that has been wound round itself. Page 21 shows you this. We can lift ourselves up easily on a screw when it is in a revolving chair.

A spoon is a machine, when you lever a tin open with it.

A ramp can be used to lift a person.

A screw makes it easy to jack up a car.

Wheels and **axles** make it easy to move large weights around. They make travelling fast and smooth. Wheels and axles on a supermarket trolley make shopping easier.

Wheels and axles make toys easy to move.

Pulling down is easier than picking up, so when you want to lift a heavy load, a rope over a strong point is an easy answer. The rope and the strong point – which can be a wheel and axle – are called a **pulley**. A pulley makes it easy to get a bucket of water.

A pulley makes lifting easy.

Lever power

Try these models with levers and pivots.

Cut the chickens and levers from thick card. Joint them with paper fasteners. Move the levers and watch the chickens peck. You may need an adult to start opening the fasteners for you.

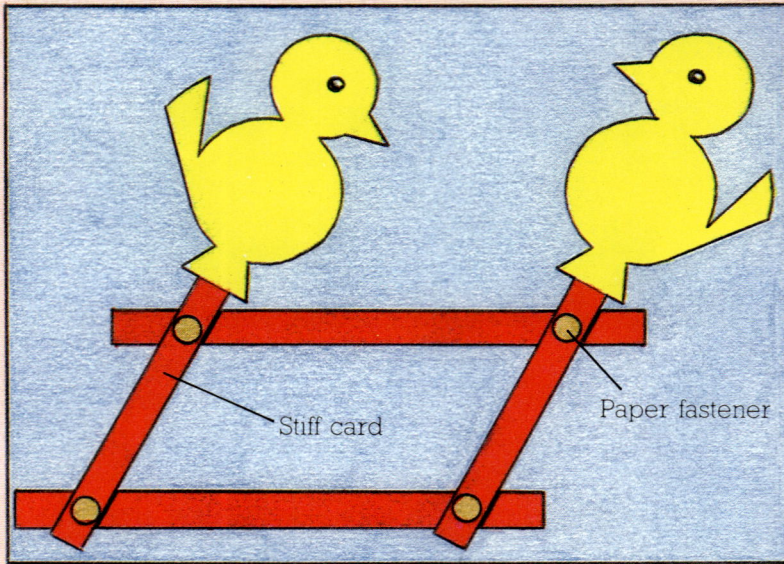

Stiff card

Paper fastener

Load

Pivot

Effort

Lever

A pivot is the point on which a lever turns.

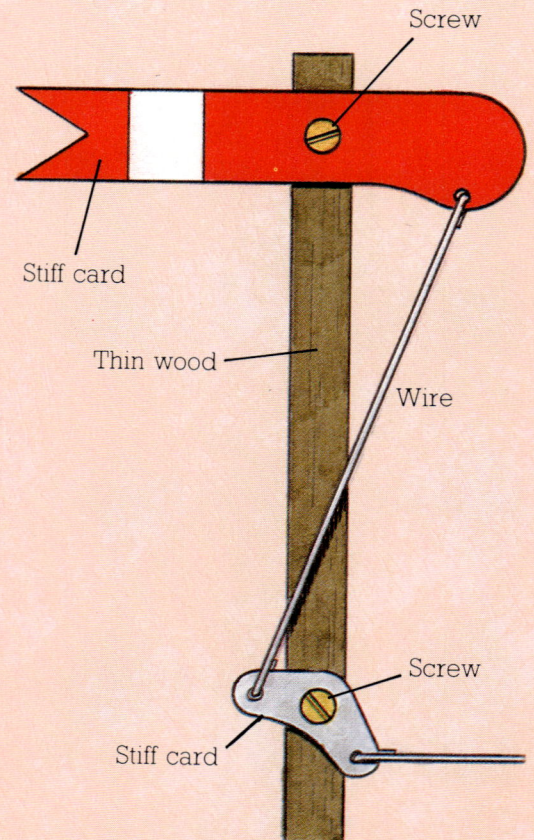

Cut the old-fashioned railway signal from thick card. You may find that only a strip of wood is stiff enough for the upright. Use florist's wire to move the signal.

Screw

Stiff card

Thin wood

Wire

Screw

Stiff card

Look around you for levers. There are many, but they are not always easy to spot.

Close the door gently by pushing the handle with one finger.

Now close the door gently by pushing the centre with one finger.

Lastly, close the door gently by pushing at the hinge end with one finger – but don't put it in the gap!

Is a door a lever?

Where is the pivot?

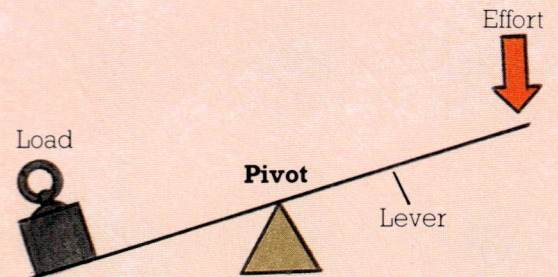

Lift that load

Ancient peoples used ramps to lift stones.

Look around you, at home, at school, or when you are out. Can you find ramps:

> in the car park?   at your school?
>
> in big stores?   in the park?
>
> in your local theatre or cinema?

Some people depend on ramps because they can't climb stairs. Most modern buildings use ramps to give disabled people access. In what other ways can disabled people move from floor to floor?

Make a paper ramp and roll it up. The edge of the paper makes a 'screw'.

You can see screws all around you: joining pieces of wood and metal, on taps and valves and on many toys.

Look at nuts and bolts of all sorts – in cars, on models and on toys.

Can you design a moving toy that:

> dances?   lifts its hat?
>
> jumps?   waves?
>
> does the splits?

Spinning wheels

We have a whole range of wheels, designed for special tasks.

What kind do you see on:

a child's bike?   a racing car?   a tractor?

Making models with wheels can be difficult. Here is one way, using the pipe insulating material you can buy at D.I.Y. shops as a tyre. Any flat box will do, but you must make holes for the axles at the *same* distances from the ends of the box. Otherwise the vehicle will not run straight.

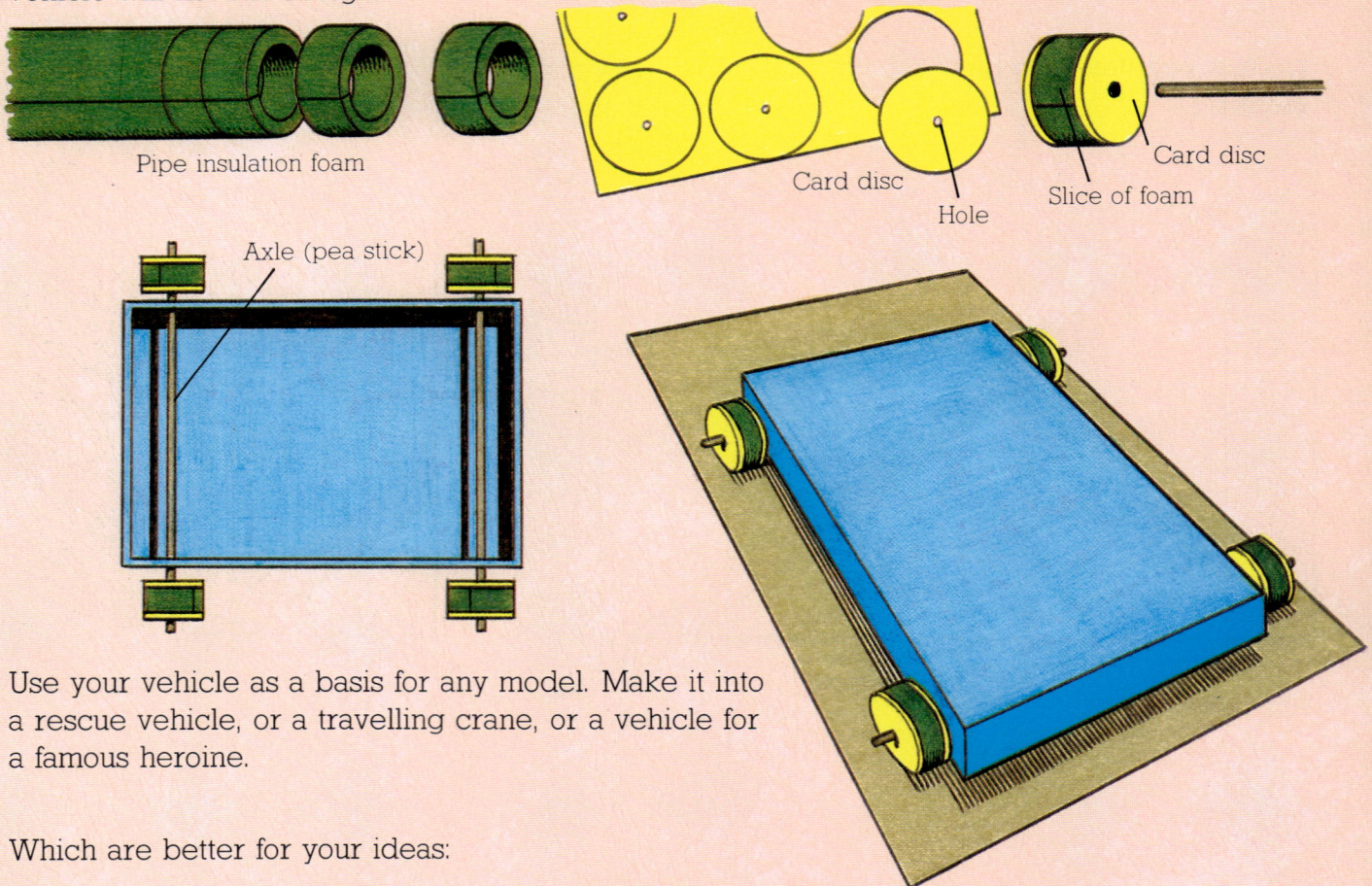

Pipe insulation foam

Card disc

Hole

Card disc

Slice of foam

Axle (pea stick)

Use your vehicle as a basis for any model. Make it into a rescue vehicle, or a travelling crane, or a vehicle for a famous heroine.

Which are better for your ideas:

wide wheels or narrow?   long axles or short?

long boxes with wheels far apart, or short boxes with wheels close together?

Can you make a vehicle that can travel one metre, and then *stop*? Think about hooks, anchors, weights and ramps.

Pulley power

You will find a pulley on a well. You will find one on a mill, or a factory wall.

Adding more ropes makes the lifting even easier. You have to pull the rope further, but the load feels lighter – as little as half the weight with two ropes, and even less with three or four ropes.

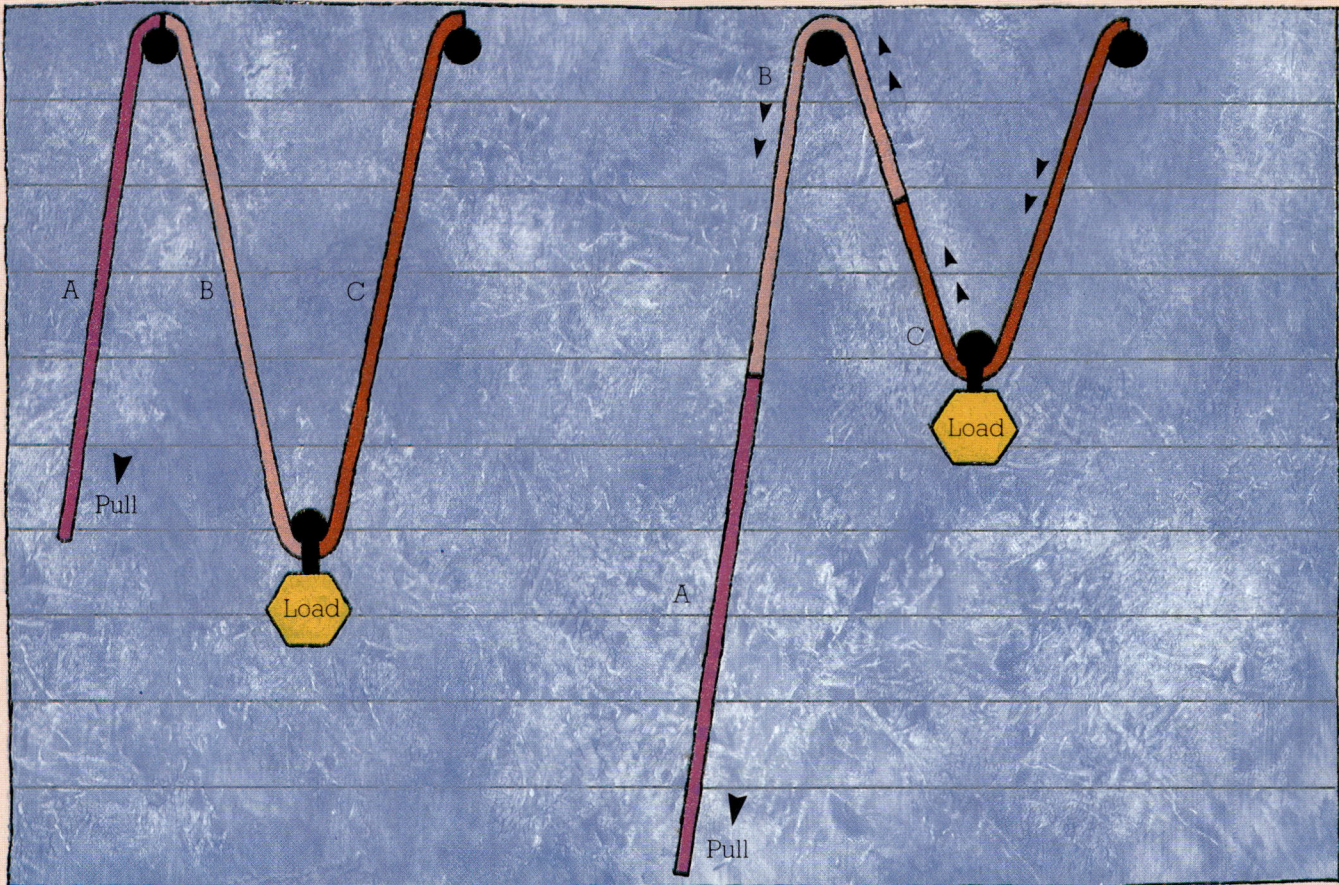

As the ropes shorten, the weight is lifted.

Rope A moves twice as far as rope B or C.

Garages use pulleys like these to lift engines.

Pulleys are used to take lifts up and down.

Can you make a pulley like these? A modelling kit like **LEGO**® or **MECCANO** may help.

Try lifting a weight with your pulley. Can you make the weight feel even lighter?

Can you fix your pulley to a crane?

Fighting friction

Many machines could work better, but they are having to overcome friction.

To understand this a little, wash your hands with soapy water, then wash them wearing rubber gloves!

The soapy water lubricates your hands. They slide easily. The rubber gloves are hard to rub together. You are working against friction.

See how a piece of scrap wood moves over different surfaces. Try it on carpet, sandpaper, a smooth board, a plastic sheet and so on.

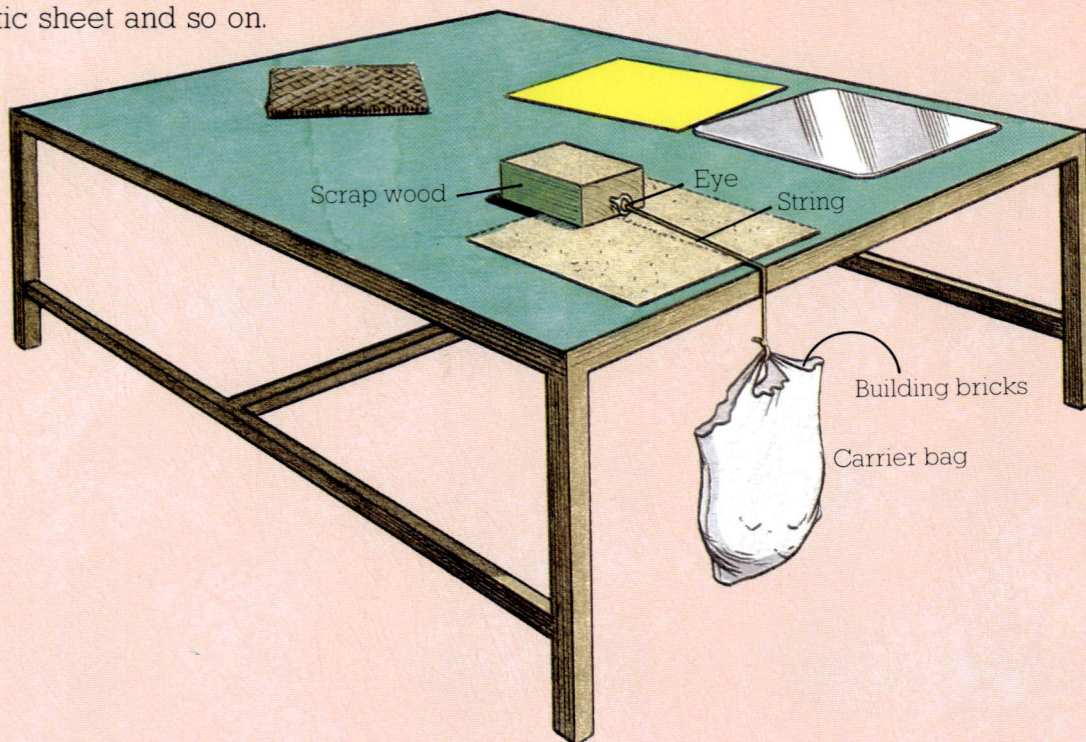

Scrap wood   Eye   String

Building bricks

Carrier bag

The weighted carrier bag shows you how hard it is to move the block. See how many bricks you can put in before the block moves.

Are smooth surfaces *always* low in friction?

Are rough surfaces *always* high in friction?

Putting on your bike brakes creates friction. But is your brake block rough? Is the wheel rough?

Does it matter how much *alike* the surfaces are?

Transmitting power

Sometimes we wish to put in effort at one point, and use it to do work at another. For this to happen, we need to **transmit** the power.

Steam train rods

There are many ways of doing this. For example:

Axles transmit the car engine's power to its wheels.

Rods transmit the power to the wheels of an old-fashioned steam train.

Chain transmits the power of your legs to a bike wheel.

A drive band transmits the power to a sewing machine.

Cogs, or gears, transmit the power to the hands of a clock.

Can you make a mechanism for transmitting power?

Bike chain

LEGO or **MECCANO** might be useful, but you could make a model using two round containers and a rubber band – your drive belt.

Can you make:
a machine that transmits power over a long distance?

a machine that uses cogs, bands, or chain to drive a wheel fast?

a machine that uses cogs, bands, or chain to drive a wheel slowly?

The more cogs, bands, or chains you introduce, the more friction may work against you. Can you feel this?

SHIPSHAPE

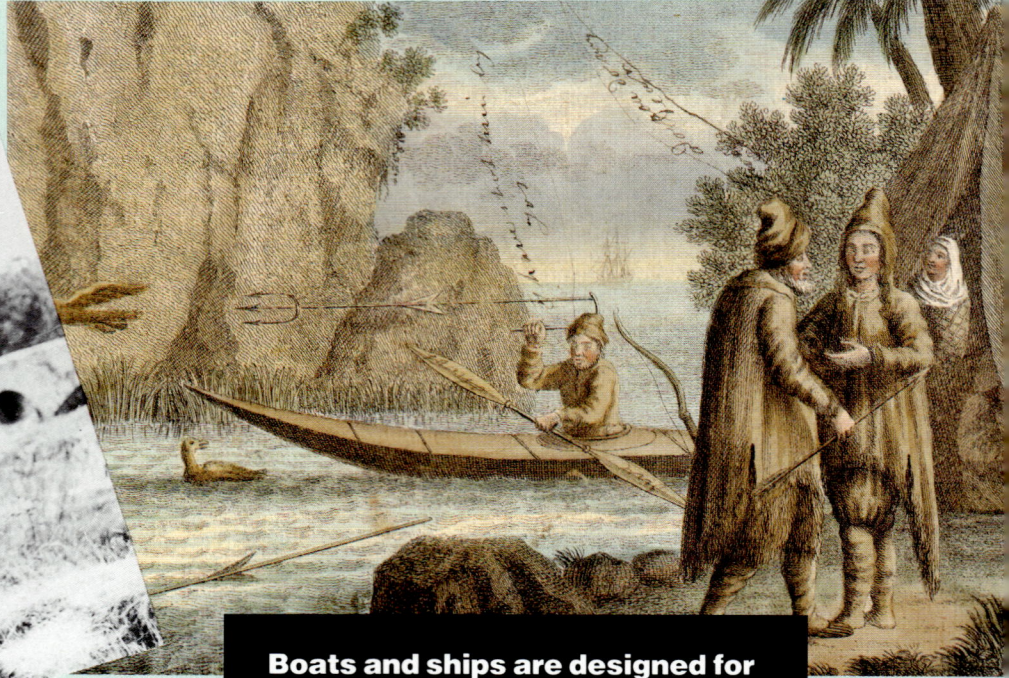

Boats and ships are designed for many different tasks. Their shape tells us about the job they do.

Boat shape!

Fast boats and ships have specially shaped hulls. The shape of the hull is important, if the boat is to move smoothly through the water.

On the left is the part of a racing yacht you don't often see; but this yacht is out of the water. Notice how smooth it is and how carefully shaped. The water will slip past it.

Here are some hull shapes, cut with a junior hacksaw from soft wood. You can think of others. Which is the best at getting through the water?

Try pulling some hulls gently through water – in the bath or a sink. Notice how the water moves round the front of the boat. Does it slip cleanly by, or is it disturbed? Does the hull stay flat, or does it rise up on the waves it is making?

Which is your best hull shape?

If you make some new hulls, all with the best front end you have discovered, does it matter how the *back* is shaped?

Look at boats in your local park or river, or in the sea if you live near it. How are they shaped?

Look under a bridge over a river or stream. How are the pillars shaped?

Boat load

You can only put so much load in a boat – too much, and it will sink.

Try this with your model hulls from page 27; or use a model boat. An empty plastic box will do.

Use a load that will not be damaged by water – plastic toys, coins, or clean stones.

How much will your boat take? Where is the best place for the load? Does it matter if you stack it up?

Try a tall plastic cup. Does it float, empty?

Does it float with:

    a small weight in it?

    a large weight in it?

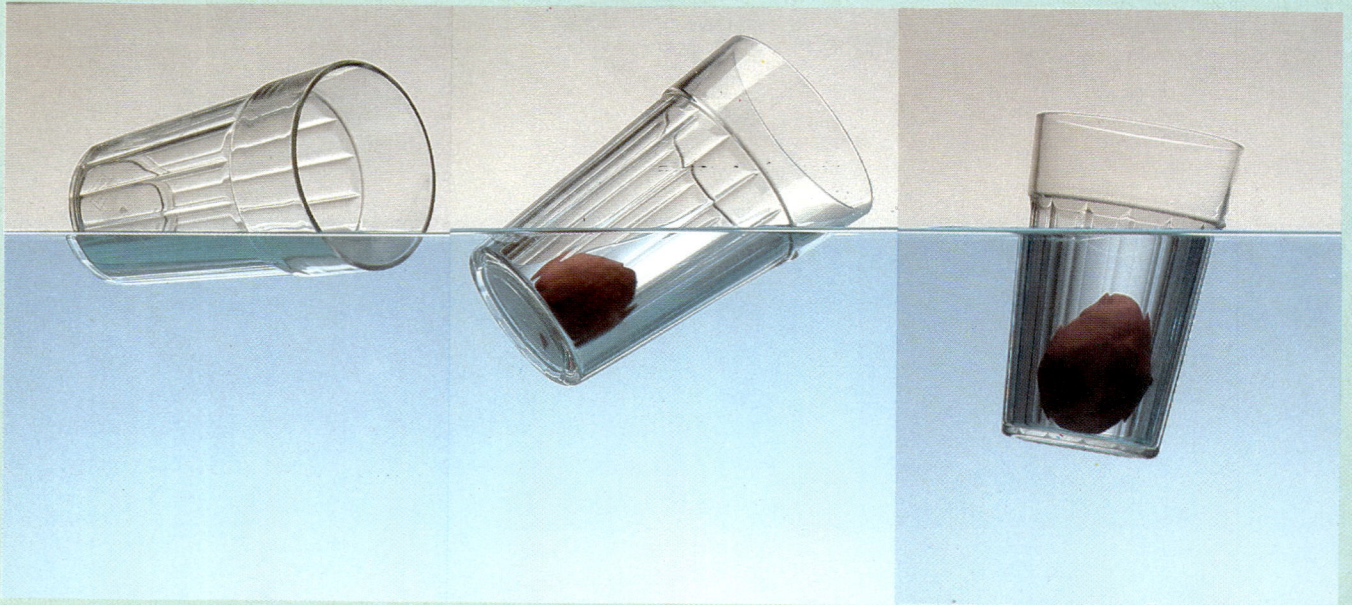

How does it float?

How high in the water is it?

Dissolve three tablespoonsful of salt in a small bowl of water. Float your tall cup in that. Try marking the water level in plain and salt water on the side of the cup. What difference is there?

Powerboats

You can row boats along or you can use the wind to push you. You can use a propeller or you can paddle the boat. Some boats use an engine to drive one or two paddle wheels.

Try this model paddleboat. Use wood. Balsa wood will be fine, but don't use thick elastic bands – they snap it. Don't leave balsa wood in water for too long, either. Why not?

Mississippi steamboat

Try different numbers of turns.

Try different sizes of elastic band.

Try different sizes of paddle.

Can you make your boat cross a bowl or bath, and stop? Experiment to find how many times you have to wind the bands, exactly.

Sail power

Many boats still use the power of the wind to move along. Wind power is free but not reliable. Early sailing boats could move when the wind was pushing them from behind but couldn't sail *into* the wind. Modern yachts can sail with the wind behind or across them.

The size and shape of a sail are important. Use a model boat to try a range of paper sails.

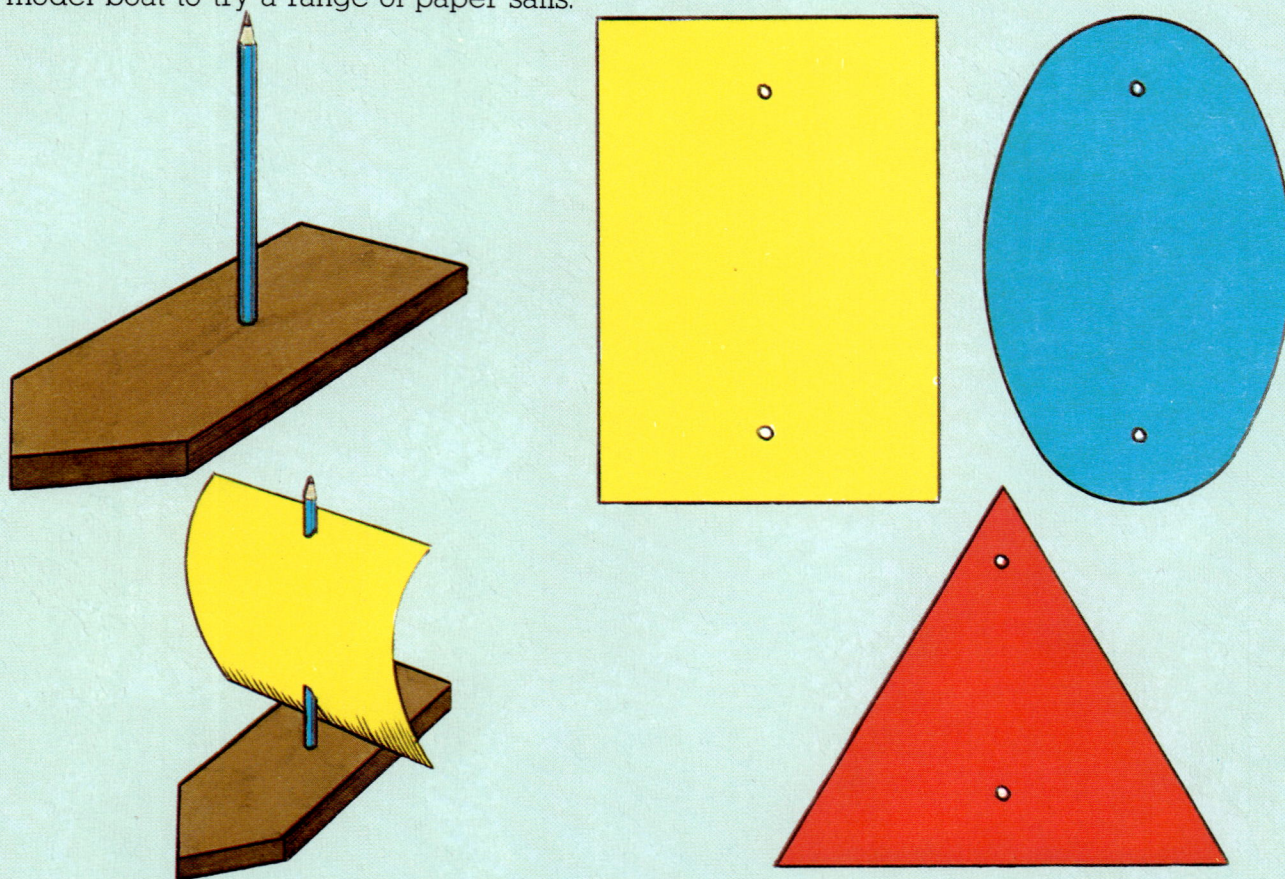

Blow with about the same strength into each of your sails in turn.

Does it matter how far away you are when you blow?

Does it matter how big the sail is?

Does it matter how far up the mast you put the sail?

Does it matter what angle the sail is at, and how curved it is?

What is the best sail to move your boat along with very little wind?

Shipshape!

There are many other ways of driving model boats. These pictures show two of them. Can you think of some more?

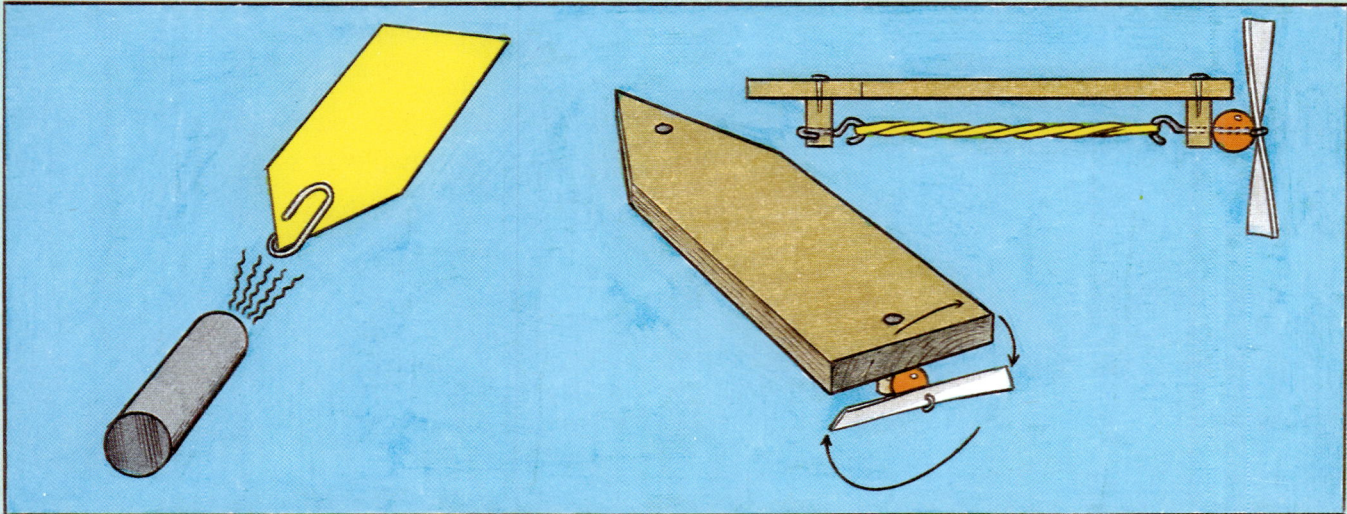

Boats spend all their time in water. Water harms some metals. Try this test to see what might happen to a boat made from the same metal as a nail.

empty

water

salt water

What happens with salt water – like a metal boat in the sea?

Can you keep the metal bright?

Does a coating help?

Try a little oil, or some house paint, or some grease or vaseline. Do they keep the metal bright?

How are metal boats kept in good condition?

Index